MW01679790

Under His Grace

Sister Shar

Thank you so much for your support

Sherry Hill

Under His Grace

By: Sherry Hill

TATE PUBLISHING
AND ENTERPRISES, LLC

Under His Grace

Published by Tate Publishing & Enterprises, LLC
127 E. Trade Center Terrace | Mustang, Oklahoma 73064 USA
1.888.361.9473 | www.tatepublishing.com

Tate Publishing is committed to excellence in the publishing industry. The company reflects the philosophy established by the founders, based on Psalm 68:11,
"The Lord gave the word and great was the company of those who published it."

Published in the United States of America

ISBN: 978-1-63306-959-6
1. Self-Help /Addictions
2. Self-Help/Recovery
14.05.19

Chapter 1

I WAS A DRUG ADDICT

Every day I would wake up, make my coffee, let the dogs out and then get high. It didn't matter what I was doing or where I was going it was the same routine. My life revolved around drugs, getting drugs, getting high and then getting more drugs. Even though I would say that I had a good life, I knew it was a lie. Every day, I lived in hiding. Nobody could know, nobody could see. It was my secret. I know now that I hated my life, that I had scars and wounds that I just wasn't dealing with, and to conceal the pain I tried to medicate myself and push the pain away. When we don't deal with our neurosis, they do not go away. They may hide, or even lull us in a sense of "I have control of this," but it's all a lie. We don't have control, it has control of us. My drug of choice was marijuana, and I really thought I had control of it because I had quit, for a month I was successful, for six months, for a year, for five years and for ten years, and the end result was I always went back. I had God, He was with me every step of the way, but obviously that was not getting me out of my addiction, I was missing something. What I was missing was exposure. It's not until I surrendered my control and allowed the truth to be told would I ever be able to get free and praise God for the victory.

And you will know the Truth, and the Truth shall make you free.

John 8:32 NKJV.

I needed freedom, and the only way to get free was to surrender and let God do whatever needed to be done. I realized my problem was more about how I dealt with the hiding than about how I dealt with the drugs. I decided to take a whole year and give God the ability to work on me and if need be, expose me. When we serve and love God, we allow Him to take control of our lives, and He helps to prune our lives in such a way, that we are ready and able to be, the Called of the Lord. I knew I didn't want to be 80 and still getting high. That was the nightmare. That life terrified me because it was all about hiding.

Exposure can be hard. Nobody likes being exposed, many times it leads to ridicule. What may not be seen, is that exposure really leads to healing and to wholeness. I wanted to be whole. I needed that desperately and I knew at that time in my life, I was not, and I was begging for healing. Only with exposure, that was out of my control, did that healing start to emerge. God had been preparing me all this time, so that when the exposure happened, I would have the strength to continue and not run from it. We run from things all the time, but running never gets us anywhere. Don't run, from your psyche. In this situation you have to stand at the door and face the fear and not run.

Behold, I stand at the door and knock. If anyone hears My voice and opens the door, I will come in to him and dine with him, and he with Me. To him who overcomes I will grant to sit with Me on My throne, as I also overcame and sat down with My Father on His throne.

Revelations 3:20-21 NKJV.

I was standing at the door and knocking wanting an answer, wanting a cure, and God heard me.

A friend of mine called and told me, Pastor knows that you're getting high, and I'm like, No Way, because that is your worst fear, along with mom and dad and the cops. As I was still on the phone talking, out of my mouth came, "whatever is hidden shall be shouted from the rooftops," and I knew this completely and honestly to be true. So later that same day I went for a bike ride and God tapped me on the shoulder and said "Go talk to Pastor." So I swing past, and he's mowing the lawn and I'm thinking great, so I come up and he doesn't shut off the mower. So I yell, "God wants me to talk to you." He looks at me and says, "I can't talk to you now," and I'm thinking, "What, you're blowing me off," and as I'm riding away I'm thinking, he knows nothing. Which of course wasn't true, because later at church he took me aside and asked "Are you still getting high," and I look at him and I'm like "Oh, you know."

My exposure was that my pastor of my church knew that I was getting high. With this knowledge I learned to be accountable for my actions. I knew he was watching, he was watching my attendance, my activity in the church, who my church friends we're, and if I was doing anything new in the church.

Many times I had thought to confide in other people, but the secret held me back. It was powerful, it controlled me. The hiding had now become an everyday defense for protection against me and the world. The hiding is what really had the control, in order to be set free, I had to break free of the hiding. I needed to understand why I was, the way I was. Was it personality, values, morals, my upbringing, ethics, the culture or just wrong decisions? It frustrated me to not know, but I knew I could go to the One who knows, Jesus Christ my savior, and Lord. So I was determined and talked with God and realized that by seeking Him diligently for this year. He would reveal to me who I was and where I was going. He would set me free and lead me into the true path, of destiny and fulfillment for my life.

Chapter 2

Hiding A Way of Life

Hiding became the natural way to live; you tell yourself it's not hiding its protection, which is the biggest lie. You're hiding from everybody, and now it's the big secret. Very, few people knew that I was a pot head. Nobody could know that. Don't you know that's the worst? It's like the biggest sin in the world, and I am still very ashamed of it. In my mind, I blew up my addiction to be the worst thing that anybody could ever do, I had to teach myself to hate the sin so that eventually a day would come, that I could use the hate to walk out of the sin.

I knew because of my faith that my addiction was a temporary trail and that if I trusted God and believed what the bible promises, God would lead me out and free me to have victory in His Name.

I had to face my biggest fear, which I thought the fear was, everybody knowing, but that was not the real fear, the real fear was failing and not succeeding to do the work and call upon my life, that I knew was possible for me. I knew the weed was holding me back. I knew it, but the addiction still had me. It wasn't letting go, and it seemed like it was stronger than ever, and I was scared, because I knew that God was allowing it, it wasn't that He set it up, but it's here and God will use a trial to make us stronger and to draw us closer to Him.

God was faithful to tell me, "Things are for a season". We all have seasons in our lives. God had warned me beforehand, so that I could prepare myself for the struggle, knowing that this was a season of pain, and allowing pain to be exposed and pain to be seen. God had warned, so that I could prepare myself for any struggle ahead. I was never initially afraid of the pain; it wasn't until I was in it, that I was afraid, but God helped me to purge the pain out and to face it with wisdom, love, and compassion. I knew that behind the weed was the pain of past experiences. Failures, lost dreams and lost hopes. The weed was my way of escaping, but praise God, with God, we don't have to escape we can confront issues and know that God will work it out for our good, if we trust in Him.

I had to be ready for the master's purpose. I had to allow myself to face the test and succeed. I had to trust in God, allow myself to be exposed, not running when it happened, and walk away from my old life and embrace the new life God had for me. I knew the new life was there, I knew it was waiting for me; all I had to do was envision it, believe it, act upon it, and watch God work.

Never before had I felt so in tune with God. I felt my spirit was growing every day, when I opened my bible, the eyes of my awareness was opened and I could read so much clearer,

God was doing a work in me and I was excited for each new day to begin. My desire for God continued to increase, as He taught me and guided me in the way I should go.

"As the plant springs from, and could not be without, the seed, so every act of a man springs from the hidden seeds of thought, and could not have appeared without them."

"As a Man Thinketh" Author James Allen

All a man's actions spring from somewhere and could not have existed without.

We all have seeds to our problems.

Is it pride, lust, revenge, all things spring from somewhere, it is in the hearts and minds of man to do evil an only with the conviction of God do we fight that, and endeavor to do good. I was winning every day. As the year continued I saw the intensity of the addiction begin to dissipate. I also identified triggers that I had, that could trigger my addiction. I knew the ability to get free and stay free was available to me, it had happened for others why not me? At this time even though I could believe it, I still couldn't see it. God assured me, that was ok, believing for right now, was key. Many have died in their addiction never believing that things would get better, I never embraced this mentality. God was here, leading and guiding, and I never lost God. If you are a person that is struggling right this minute, seek out God, in any way you can. Music, church, the word, whatever you gravitate towards, you seek it, and God will meet you.

"And therefore the Lord earnestly waits, expecting, looking, and longing to be gracious to you; and therefore He lifts Himself up, that He may have mercy on you, and show loving-kindness to you. For the Lord is a God of justice. Blessed (happy, fortunate, to be envied) are all those who earnestly wait for Him, who expect look and long for Him, for His victory, His favor, His love, His peace, His joy and His matchless unbroken companionship."

Isaiah 30:18 Amplified Bible

Chapter 3

Stuck

Every day I just felt stuck, I felt powerless and out of control, I felt like the addiction had me and was sucking the life out of me, and I was doing everything, I could think of to do, to break out of its control. I thought the control was all powerful, but I learned more than anything, it is our lives that are more powerful, our dreams our visions, our goals. These are the things that I now know define our purpose, because without purpose we're all lost. God gives us that purpose, and you see it, with others that have died, they had purpose, but they were blind to it. I am so thankful today that we serve a God that is faithful to His word, where He gives us guidance and direction and purpose for our lives, but only if we reach out and grab it. I have learned, if I do not grab it, then the addiction has the control, and I have no control. Maybe there are some of you that feel like you have lost your purpose, well then you need to find it, and if you have an inkling and it's the opposite of something you have never done, then you go with that, and see what God does. Sometimes we have to do something completely different or we will continue to stay stuck. I wanted to have control of my addiction and I was seeking any means, be it exposure, confrontation, surrender, study or prayer. I was not going to stop until the victory was mine; I was going to get free and stay free and teach others to stay free. No more lying, no more hiding, no more. I was going to be in control and I was going to walk strong and believe God, that there was a time, a day and an hour, in which I would walk out free, and never look back on a life of misery. Who's standing in line for that life? Nobody, and we mourn for the one's we have lost, that life, can only steal and rob from us.

Chapter 4

Lies

I lied to people every day, it was the only way I knew how to live, to protect the secret. I wasn't getting caught, I wasn't doing anything so overt to draw attention to myself, but I was still living a life of lies, hiding and fear. It was only when I started crying out to God that exposure came in and the lies were uncovered, after that I realized the lies had no meaning or hold on me, and I started to walk forward in honesty and truth. God was changing me and I was becoming the person I had always wanted to be.

A friend of mine once told me, "That with God, you never have to lie", which is very true. Even though I embraced that, and kept that saying, it took me awhile to actually walk in it, and I can say today that I have more victory in that area than ever before. If we allow the lies to control us and to dictate to us how to live, then the lie has the control, and we have sunk deeper into our addiction. The lies can never give us freedom, it is only by seeking the truth can we ever be free. The truth can be scary, I was concerned for my family, my friends and others on how they would respond, but I knew I could not quit, I could not go back and that if I kept going forward then God would make it alright and give me a new life of joy and happiness. We all want these things, but are we willing to make the hard choices to get them. I was, and all I could do was pray that people would give me mercy and forgiveness. If we are not careful the fear of the unknown can stop us, but I refused to let it stop me. I knew what God was telling me, and I had to believe that in the end it would work out far better than I could ever envision.

Chapter 5

Failure

Sometimes I felt like such a failure, failure as a Christian, failure as a parent and failure as a daughter. I felt so worthless; I'm getting high every day and I'm not stopping. I wanted to stop; I needed to stop, but it was not happening. On many days, I wanted to push myself to do so much better, but God was here, and I knew I was just getting caught up in the flesh, just wanting to do anything but not necessarily the right thing. I knew the right thing to do was to, "Stand still and see the salvation of the Lord." Sometimes to just stand still and do nothing can be the hardest thing, because it takes the action out of our hands and allows God to act. When God acts He does it right, it is up to us, as believers to give God time, and for us to follow as sheep, trusting and leaning on the Shepherd, and knowing that He will guide us safely home. I wanted safety, I wanted freedom but I just didn't know how to get it. All I knew to do was to pray, seek God diligently and attend my church and give God time to work on my behalf. It may seem to you during this time that nothing is happening, but I know in my own life during this time, that God was working, my mind was changing and I was changing. Yes, the drugs where still there every day, but I was getting better. Don't let the devil lie to you and tell you that you are a failure during this time because you're not. Many think, that we all have to go cold turkey, to get free. I had done this so many times I wanted to scream, because it just wasn't working for me. The only steps that I knew to take were to lean on God, expose myself, stand still, confront what I needed to confront and believe. As I gained victory, I started distancing myself from that environment.

I didn't seek it out, and in time I didn't even crave it. Is that to say I never went through a period of craving? No many times I would hit rock bottom. I went through a really rough patch, where nobody would help me and when they did, I'd get ripped off. I was crying every day and the reason, is that I was in trouble and nobody would help me. Now I know, it was a blessing, because I didn't need help in that area, it was really an act of tough love. Today I praise God, because I had to go through all these steps to get free. Even though after this struggle, I did go back to getting high the, intensity of it diminished. I was feeling more in control, my resolve was stronger than ever before and I was ashamed of how I had acted during that time period. I didn't like that person at all and wanted to never be that person again. That person was scared, lonely and pathetic, who wants to be that person? I didn't, and neither does God. He wants us to rise above our problems even when we're in the middle of them. I was in the middle every day, but I knew there was a way out. I knew that God was leading and freedom was just down the road. The path I was on was dark and scary, but I refused to run and go back, I knew by going forward, I would come to a day of freedom and victory.

Chapter 6

The Truth

It's not that our own truth will set us free, because our own truth may be flawed; it's that Gods truth is always perfect, and He knows the path we must go to get the victory. Isn't that what you want, victory for your life? I did, I had dreams, I had plans, but I knew that my addiction would hold me back and that if I didn't get free, I had the potential to hurt a lot of people by lying. I was tired of lying, I was tired of hiding, and I was so tired of the weed. Out of my mouth I would say, "It steals my peace, it steals my health and it steals my wealth." It really did, it stole from me every day. I wanted to end the cycle. I knew I could only do it with God's help.

Praise God in His infinite wisdom told me, "There is a way, a day and a time that you can walk out of this addiction".

Don't you know that God holds the world around us? He is the creator of all, and He holds our world, especially when we give it to Him freely. I knew that He held my world. When you are exposed and your secret is shouted from the rooftops even if there is only one person to hear, you come to a crossroads where you have to make a decisive decision. Not just a decision, a decisive decision, where study and thought have to go into it. I came to that crossroads. When I did, that didn't mean I automatically stopped smoking but now because my thoughts were lined up with God, with the word and with my own knowledge that "I would quit forever," my next thought or action would be to curtail in time that activity, and eventually be set free and never return by the grace of God, always understanding that it was never me, but God's hand holding me up. Now in the past had I never asked to be set free? I had, but now because I was totally surrendering everything unto God. He could come in with His power and strength to lift me out of my addiction and do a work in me.

***"Your right hand, O Lord,
has become glorious in power;***

***Your right hand, O Lord,
has dashed the enemy in pieces."***

Exodus 15:6 NKJV

The work that God did was for me to come out of hiding, and allow others to see, that I had an addiction. At first all who saw where my other drug friends, then I allowed myself to be exposed to my best friend, who was truly a friend, never judging me and loving me through it all, then my Pastor and then more. After that the pressure from God to do the book was easy. At another time I had felt God tell me to write about my addiction and I had refused or had hid it in my writings to represent something else, never the entire truth was revealed until now. Now I wanted to share my struggle with others and felt that this was now a God thing, and that God would use this to help other Christian's who were struggling to get free and not knowing, why they couldn't. As a Christian we are taught, "You're not praying enough, you haven't repented enough", which is a lie, because we have, never realizing a very important piece of the puzzle was missing and that was the exposure. I knew that I was getting free every day, I would get up and feel refreshed and energized to start the day, I felt I had purpose, I had renewed energy to write and as the words filled the page I could feel the presence of God infilling me and making me stronger to be the person I had always prayed and hoped to be. The addiction will never let you truly be you. The addiction will control and warp you, and for some it will even kill. Don't let this happen to you, let God lift you out of your addiction. Believe it, and it can happen for you, just as it did for me.

Chapter 7

No Where To Run

We have to get to the point where we refuse to run and hide any more. We run from the blame and blame others; we run from the pain and bury it, never allowing ourselves to feel the hurt and misery. We run from confrontation never wanting to stand up for ourselves and possibly anger another. We have to come to the conviction that what I'm doing or have done is not working and then take a leap of faith and do something different. This can be scary for some, but I will tell you that moving in a direction helps God to work. Lying there doing nothing will only feed the addiction. Many times I would come to a wall, but you know what I would do, I would study harder, pray harder, listen to my Christian music louder and praise God through it all. Yes I would get free only to lose it and fall back, wanting to beat myself up over it, only to have God say, "Learn something from this", and I would. One lesson I learned is that when you're craving but not wanting, you don't call a drug friend, you find an advocate to call to help you. Of course by calling an advocate I was once again exposing myself, but that's when healing would rush in. Is it easy, no it is hard. I won't lie to you, changing our life is hard, but it's worth it. Don't you want to be free and happy and on your way. That's what God wants for you, but we have to fight for it. We know how to fight and we will fight for a cause. Isn't your life cause enough, aren't your children cause enough. Find a cause and you fight for it, and that will lead you out of your addiction, it did me.

Chapter 8

Failed Again

What happens when we fail again? Does that mean it's over? Some of you are saying "yes it's over". No it's not.

We all fail, but failure does not have to define our life. God taught me that. I failed and failed and failed again and every time I pressed into God, I pressed into life, I pressed into wholeness. Dwelling on the failure made me miserable and I wanted to be happy, so I picked myself up and would start working on my freedom once again. Did freedom come the very next day, no, but I knew I would learn, I would grow and when the addiction dissipated, I would make better and wiser choices than before, and be stronger. That's what we never see, is our increased strength. The devil will lie to you and tell you, you're not getting stronger, but I can assure you, you are. Any time we work towards a goal, eventually change will come in, and if the change is slow. Praise God you're still changing. Don't worry about the time frame that's in God's hands. I always believed that God would get me out of my addiction. All I had to do, was to never let go of God. It was God leading and guiding me. Making me stronger and increasing my self-worth, increasing my belief and my faith, that a day was coming in which I would be totally free and walk in the victory God had for me. If today you feel like you cannot believe that you can get free, I can assure you, you are wrong.

Chapter 9

You Can't Get Here

From There

When we look at our lives and see our potential we realize that to get somewhere we have to be on the right path. The right path can lead us home, the right path can lead us to our destiny, and the right path is a God path, which is full of blessings and purpose. If we lose our path we have to work hard to get back on it, but nothing is ever impossible, and God makes all things possible for the child that believes. If all you can do today is believe for a brighter future then you go with that, and I assure you that in time your belief will increase even if you're in the middle of your addiction, you can have that belief, because I did. I knew I had to be in the middle in order to get out. So many times I would make it to the middle and want to run, but I knew from past experience if I ran, then the addiction got stronger and I got weaker. I learned at this time to not run, to not run from the confrontation, but to expose it, and triumph over it. During this time I learned, that if I was in a verbal fight with someone, to not be the person to leave in a huff, because either way you're still fighting with the person in your mind as you walk away. I learned to stand there and finish the fight and then to walk away with more clarity and more power.

I knew that this was not the life I wanted to be in. This life was sorrow and pain and hiding and lying. This life was misery. I had the knowledge of knowing that I could never get to my destiny if I took this path, and neither can you. It is not only God leading us during this time, but it's our knowledge of past failures, and experiences, that would be the catalyst to help me to make wiser and more decisive decision's, that would change my life forever. At this time I worked very hard to get the weed out of my house and off my person, I had places I could go to and get it, and never return with it home. I isolated my home and everyday life from the weed, and only relegated specific places that it was available. When I needed weed I would go to those places, where I knew it was available and then later was able to walk away and return home free. I remember walking into my home and being so happy that at least here I was free of the addiction, even if I was still running to places to get it, I knew I was gaining in freedom and that eventually I would of my own accord and circumstances make the decision to never return to a life of misery. It is only when we start limiting ourselves, that more limits will come in, and then we can walk free into victory and newness of life.

Chapter 10

Peace

Never before had I felt the presence of God more than during this trial, I knew I could not succeed without God's help, and I wanted so desperately to get well. I knew my way of doing it had not worked, I had tried everything, but what I had not tried was consecration. I needed to get quiet and calm and to allow peace to be the ruler of my heart. Peace is a presence that can be invoked, studied, felt, and enjoyed. If you are not enjoying peace today then you need to seek it. Seek it with a whole heart and peace will come to you, but always knowing that peace can never happen with discord, it is only with a repentant heart do we receive.

I knew every day I was getting better, my life was unfolding for me and I was no longer walking scared, but now God was here teaching me to walk with courage, integrity, and discipline. If you are a person today that lacks these qualities, I am here to tell you, that with time, study and God, you can receive them. God is no respecter of persons, what He does for one; He will do for the other. God has such a wonderful plan for all of us, but we have to have the courage and wisdom to find it, and to seek it with a whole heart. The bible says "that with fear and trembling do we seek out our own salvation", really what that is saying, is that we seek out our life, and our life unfolds for us, if we use wisdom as a dictator. Our life is made up of our everyday choices and we choose every day, with the knowledge and environment that we are placed in, but if you're like me I was always trying to change my life for a better life than I or my parents had. We see what can be available to us if we walk in wisdom, we know that good is available and freedom is available. So why do people miss it? Fear is number one, if you allow the fear to dictate, you will not do the hard work that needs to be done to get free, but Good News, when you invoke peace fear has to go.

Chapter 11

Freedom

The day of my freedom was set by God. If I continued to walk and trust in Him, then He would lead me to freedom and when that freedom came, I embraced it and never looked back. I had heard various sermons throughout my trail, one said to starve an addiction, which really is going cold turkey, this may work for you, but it didn't for me, another said to flee. I had never heard this before concerning an addiction, but really what it said, was to flee to a safe place where healing could come in. I decided that I needed to get myself safe, and cloistered with God. To receive from Him, I needed to have advocates that I could talk to and turn to, and that if I failed, I could lean into God, trusting in Him for the victory again, but now using the failure as a catalase that would propel me towards wholeness and health. That's what I wanted and was striving for. If today you can't believe for yourself, believe it for the children that will come after you, ones that we don't want exposed to this lifestyle. This is not an attractive lifestyle, it kills and it destroys and I was tired of it destroying my life, and I was not going to keep on giving it power. God has given you the power to have victory, but you have to reach out and take it.

For no temptation (no trial regarded as enticing to sin, no matter how it comes or where it leads) has overtaken you and laid hold on you that is not common to man [that is, no temptation or trial has come to you that is beyond human resistance and that is not adjusted and adapted and belonging to human experience, and such as man can bear]. But God is faithful [to His Word and to His compassionate nature], and He [can be trusted] not to let you be tempted and tried and assayed beyond your ability and strength of resistance and power to endure, but with the temptation He will [always] also provide the way out (the means of escape to a landing place), that you may be capable and strong and powerful to bear up under it patiently.

I Corinthians 10:12 (Amplified Bible)

When we seek a landing place of rest and safety we are hindering the addictive control on us and allowing a spiritual control to take over. Every day I was seeking out God, having better attendance at church, attending bible studies, fellowship with Christian friends, reading and studying my bible, participating in group or individual prayer. I knew I had to reach out to others for help. This was very hard for me, I am a private person, but I knew I could not succeed in isolation it was only in confrontation and exposure that I would be healed. The person who I ultimately sought out was a person that knew about the addiction, and that I felt I could trust and ask to be an advocate. We all need advocates, someone who we can turn to when the desire gets strong. I can remember times when I was driving to get high with tears streaming down my face because a part of me didn't want it. As we get stronger and the desire to quit increases it may seem for a time that things have gotten worse but really everyday you're getting better because you've come to the decision to quit and get free. If you keep on the path no demon in hell or on earth can stop you from getting your victory.

Chapter 12

My Pastor

The church that I was going to helped me tremendously. No one ever knew that I was getting high, my pastor knew and I believe he took great pains to cover my sin and to speak from the pulpit to encourage me, to direct me and to help me find strength to have the victory. I believe he saw my struggle and pain, but out of love and compassion he covered me and prayed for me. I never felt judged by him or rejected. Instead I felt accepted and loved. When you are in the middle of your addiction it is so important to seek out those that will encourage you and love you without fault or reservation. This is a time of being exposed and allowing the pain to be revealed and dealt with. I couldn't run from my pastor, he knew, he showed me that I didn't have to be scared. That he would keep my secret until I was able to get free and reveal it myself. I did not want my life to be a lie, a life of hiding and never getting free. I wanted freedom and I knew that I was on the right path, it was a hard path but a path that I knew would hold great dividends. I couldn't continue to live a lie, it was ripping me apart and I knew that if I did not quit, the suffering that I was experiencing would then spread to others. It has always been my desire to protect others and shelter them from my addiction. I did not want them to be hurt because of my lack of strength.

This poem really spoke to me and showed me that this is who I wanted to be, and I would read it and believe that this is who I could be.

"I have to live with myself and so

I want to be fit for myself to know;

Always to look myself straight in the eye.
I don't want to stand with the setting sun And
hate myself for the things I've done, I want to go
out with my head erect; I want to deserve all
men respect; But here in the struggle for frame
and pelf. I want to be able to like myself.

I don't want to think as I come and go That I'm
bluster and bluff and empty-show.

I never can hide myself from me,

I see what others may never see,

I know what others may never know,

I never can fool myself, and so

Whatever happens I want to be

Self-respecting and conscience-free."

Edgar A. Guest

I knew that God would lead me out of my addiction and give me the strength and fortitude to walk in victory and to be able to teach others by my own struggle.

No matter what, Never, Never, Never give up, freedom is right around the corner, walk in it and it can be yours. Don't lose heart. I'm cheering you on for your own success. God loves you and so do I. Keep on moving in the direction of your victory and it will not fail you. If you fail get up and try again.

Chapter 13

Persevering

Every day was a struggle to get free and stay free, but I also knew to do this without God I would be lost. I knew that in time, if I just stayed on this path that I would get free and stay free and that a new me would emerge that would see my past and not be dictated by it. If I preserved and held strong even when all hell was breaking loose the addiction would dissipate and victory would be my reward. Persevering would help me to get strong and to walk out of my addiction. I knew that because I had God on my side, even when it looked like nobody else was there, that God would guide me and lead me, but that I had to be like a sheep being led by the shepherd, being docile, and obeying and that if I stumbled or got lost He would come and find me and set me on the right path again. As the year continue to unfold and got closer to completion I could see the end and when the end came I knew I would be ready for it and never again turn back to a life of misery and pain. Sometimes when we fail it's because God is leading us to a saturation point where we see the evil and despair of our lives and that is when we start digging ourselves out. We see that we have to prune off the deadness of our life. You may have to prune off friends. One reason I believe I kept going back was because I had never completely pruned myself from my drug friends. I am a very loyal person and will hang on to people because of that loyalty. In my situation that loyalty was slowly being eroded and when the final break happened I saw it as a gift and was able to eventually walk away. I knew that I could not look back, I was not going to run back and repair the breach, all this was happening to set me free and the gift, God was giving me was that I could now walk in victory and newness of life. When we take a stand to change our lives we must be willing to turn and walk in a new direction, to not back track but to raise ourselves up on a higher plateau looking forward and tackling life with strength, fortitude and energy and knowing that God is leading and we can walk into a new life that had always been planned for us.

Chapter 14

Independence Day

A day was coming in which I would be free from this addiction, an Independence Day of not only drugs, but from fear, insecurity, loss and pain, a day of freedom and renewed life for me to walk in. The weed was only a symptom of a deeper problem, a problem of my own neurosis. What was I running from? What was I scared of and how was all this controlling me and shaping me into the person I am? Not necessarily the person I want to be but who I was today. We all have an ideal of what type of person we want to be, but my ideal, I felt actually could be reality. Every day I prayed to get better, nicer and wiser. I knew I didn't want to hurt people only help them. As Christians we are taught to be Christ-like, to be like Jesus, to have compassion, mercy, love and kindness. I desired these things, I wanted these things and I knew only with God's help could I have and display these attributes. Every day God is trying to mold us, and we can either help or hinder the process. I did not want to be fighting God. If you are today fighting the process you are in fact fighting God.

Casting the whole of your care [all your anxieties, all your worries, all your concerns, once and for all] on Him, for He cares for you affectionately and cares about you watchfully.

I Peter 5:7 (Amplified Bible)

One way to know if you are fighting God is to ask yourself, “am I frustrated.” When we are frustrated we have turned away from God and are not trusting and adhering to His ways. Remember God is always patient and kind; He is a God of justice, and righteousness, a God that deals with us fairly. If today you would reach out to Him, and surrender yourself to Him, He would infuse you with His peace, and love. Not our peace, not our love because it is flawed, but God’s is perfect and never ending.

Chapter 15

Sometimes

Sometimes you have to let things go, sometime you have to say I'm sorry, sometimes you have to forgive and sometimes you have to encourage. I don't always do this, sometimes I do this very wrong and I pick myself up and I ask God to help me again, and He does. I hurt people and am so busy, that I don't even know it. I treat people with civility, but not necessarily niceness. When we walk into a room, we can walk in silent, civil, nice, very nice or very very nice. Why do we have levels? It's the amount of trust that we have in each situation, which opens us up and puts us at each level.

Sometimes we have to be open to opportunities in our lives that can help us and change us for the better. If we do not allow ourselves to be open and expecting then we limit ourselves to the same old routine and life can then get pretty dull and boring, maybe for you it's just making a phone call to that person that is on your mind, maybe it's going back to school, or taking that part-time job, these are small things that will change your life and make it better. You have to make a commitment to distance yourself from your addiction. In the beginning it will be hard because you still want it, it's not about instantaneous freedom; it's about making a decision to get free and then working towards that goal. Anytime we can fill up our lives with other activities besides the addiction then it helps us to have distance and with distance you will have freedom. It has happened for me why not you.

Chapter 16

In the Land of Anxiety

I suffer from anxiety. I asked myself, anxiety what is this? It can be defined as, a painful or apprehensive uneasiness of mind, over impending or anticipated harm, having fearful concern. I know now I have this. It is also defined as an abnormal and overwhelming sense of apprehension or fear and doubt concerning the reality and nature of a threat.

I asked myself, so what does this mean? I know I have fear in my life, I have doubts, but it said an easiness of mind. So my mind is fearful and because of that it causes uneasiness in my being. This uneasiness is due to some threat of harm to me? What harm? Possibly if I do it right there will be no harm, but if I do it wrong, harm will ensue.

It is also defined by self-doubt about one's capacity to cope with harm? The more and more I juggle this around the more and more I got confused. God is not the author of confusion. So I knew that God would explain it to me,

He'd get me a good book, I'd read an article and knowledge would come in, and I would understand completely what I had and I didn't need to worry with God around. My addiction was a result of my anxiety. I turned towards drugs to alleviate my fear and any threat of fear, but this is a lie. Drugs in themselves weaken us, they control us and they can harm and kill us. Anxiety will not kill you, initially this heightened awareness helps us to flee danger, but now in our day and age anxiety is an unhealthy coping mechanism that we use to alleviate fear. I asked myself, how do we get rid of fear? I learned it is by confronting it, there is no other way, and when you confront fear, endurance comes in. Courage has been described as action even when fear is present. By acting we are controlling the fear and walking through it. Many of us fear loss and separation, but live in separation every day. Why are we so separate? Why are we so disjointed, you're here, I'm over there, and when we are together we are still distant. It always has to start with one. Just one, who is willing to not allow distance to dictate, look at the friends you already have, and get closer to them, family, church, school, exercise class. You be the one to make the difference. So I decided to do this, I had to be the one to have a closer relationship with my sister, a closer relationship with my friends, a closer relationship with my son. It had to be up to me, nobody else, just me, doing the work and believing in God that my relationships could change.

It wasn't that I had terrible relationships, I had good relationships, but don't you want better? I did. If today you will confront the fear, with God's help we can overcome, I have and so can you.

Chapter 17

Hate is a word

I hated myself because I got high, I hated that it stole from me my peace, my strength and my breath. Every day you're getting up to attack your body with substances that are harmful, poisonous, altering and irreversible. I was crying every day because I hated the weed. I didn't want it, but it sure wanted me. I felt so powerless against it, but I also knew that the year was not over and in this year, I would have to face and bear the struggle and not turn, that only by facing it would I ever be able to get free and stay free. I never allowed hate to take over, people will say, I hate myself; I never did this I hated the weed, I hated the addiction, I hated the lying. Don't let your hate be internalized, see it as a foreign agent that with time, love and faith you can defeat. You have to look deep inside yourself and figure out what triggers the hate that you have inside yourself and see it now as something that can be changed and to start loving yourself, when we do this the devil cannot steal from us, we now are taking back our self-control, our self-worth and our self-esteem. It is easy? No its not, but I can assure you it's worth it. By taking back your control you are every day getting stronger and the addiction is getting weaker.

Chapter 18

Pruning Your Life

We all need to prune our lives. I came to the real awareness that I needed to prune my friends, this was really hard for me. I have a tendency to hang on to my friends, it's only when they dump me do I then prune them out of my life. God showed me something about loyalty, when people watch a football game different loyalties will come out. One person is like me, if the team is doing badly, I'm still cheering for them down to the wire. Another, only has loyalty when the team is doing well, if they start to lose then the disrespect will come out. You have to ask yourself is the second person really loyal or are they tossed to and fro with the direction of the game? Even though I could see the benefit in pruning, I still had soul ties to these people, and something was making me hang on to them. The only thing I knew; was it had to be the drugs always pulling me back and not necessarily the people. It was not about me dealing with the people, it was me dealing with the drugs. Once I was able to deal with my addiction then I found that it was easier to let go of those people that were holding me back and turn to the ones that were building me up. You can do this also, and I can assure you it will take time, but what you will find, is that your true friends will also be your biggest advocates.

Chapter 19

At A Cross Roads

We will all come to a crossroads. Every day that we live we are moving in some direction. I wanted to always be moving into a direction of more abundance. More friends more clean living and yes more money, but money can't be everything, it is a tool that we use to enhance our lives. If you allow it to be anything else; then it controls us, and can make our lives miserable. You may come to a cross roads with Christ. Where you realize you need more of God. When I wanted more of God, I found good authors, Joyce Meyer, Madam Guyon, and James Allen. Their books changed my life and helped me to grow. A cross roads, is really a growing opportunity, that leads us towards maturity, as long as we don't run away. If you run, there will just be another cross roads down the way waiting for you. I had run so many times and always I found that the situation always just kept coming back. Until we deal with our problems they will not go away, and if you're like me. I found I was dealing with what I thought was the problem, only to find out it was not the real problem. Our problems many times will have many layers and we have to be willing to go deep enough to decipher what is the real problem, until we do that we will only be dealing with the symptoms. Please today seek out what the real problem is, and it may hide, you may have to seek it out with courage and determination, but I assure you, you will be rewarded with an answer.

Chapter 20

Problems and Troubles

Have you ever heard the saying "Nobody knows, the trouble I've seen," this was actually in a song, by Louis Armstrong. It gives us a clue about ourselves. Problems and troubles come two ways, they are either placed upon us, or we engage them, one is no fault of our own and the other is our entire fault, but that never means that we can't change it. We do have options, we can get better, we can seek out friends to help us, and we can seek out God. He will never forsake us.

"...I will never leave you nor forsake you..."

Hebrews 13:5 NKJ

God is always there leading and guiding us into a better life and a renewed hope. If all today you have is hope, for a better life, then I can assure you that you are on your way. Many times when I was in the middle of my addiction all

I had was hope, yes I still was getting high every day but I knew that hope would lead me out and lead me through. Never give up on hope it is a force and a weapon that we have as God's children to carry us when nothing else will. We must never give up on hope, even when everything around us is falling apart we can have hope for a better tomorrow, a better future, and a better life. Hope never fails us. It is only when we become hopeless that we fail, but good news God is here to lead and guide us.

Psalms 71:1-2,5

In You O Lord, do I put my trust and confidently take refuge; let me never be put to shame or confusion!

Deliver me in Your righteousness and cause me to escape; bow down Your ear to me and save me!

FFor you are my hope; O Lord God, You are my trust from my youth and the source of my confidence.

Amplified Bible

Chapter 21

Never Giving Up

I was determined that I would never give up, that I would succeed and that I would get free. As I am writing this, the year has come and gone and I am walking in true freedom. I was so scared that this day would not come, I was so sure that I was weak and the addiction was stronger, but it was all a lie. I never gave up, I hurt sometimes so bad, and I failed miserable, but God, yes God had mandated that I would be free and I was determined to never let go of God, and now today I'm in a new year and my addiction is gone, and it will never return. I have learned diligence, I have learned confrontation and I have learned separation. All these help, me to retain my freedom and make me stronger. I have pruned my life, old friends are gone, new friends have emerged that keep me strong and the truth has now been revealed. Exposure has come in and illuminated my entire life for all to see, no more hiding, no more lying and no more weed. It has been eradicated and eliminated from my life and I work every day to maintain it. I have knowledge of what I can do and what I cannot do. I know what my triggers are and I don't allow myself to get into situations or around people that would trigger my addiction. I have allowed myself to experience the pain, no longer running or hiding, but now embracing it and walking through it. I have taken off the blinders and now I see. Is it all pretty? No, many times it is very ugly, but I have allowed myself to see the true me and to love myself exposing all my faults and with God's guidance learning to live in a new world of freedom, truth and accountability.

Chapter 22

All Has Been Heard

"All has been heard; the end of the matter is: Fear God [revere and worship Him, knowing that He is] and keep His commandments, for this is the whole of man [the full, original purpose of his creation, the object of God's providence, the root of character, the foundation of all happiness, the adjustment to all inharmonious circumstances and conditions under the sun] and the whole [duty] for every man. For God shall bring every work into judgment, and every secret thing, whether it is good or evil. "

Ecclesiastes 12:13-14 Amplified Bible

I no longer walk in fear every single day; I have been totally set free. God has brought all things to pass. I know that I am "a new creature in Christ." I walk forward everyday with renewed purpose and energy. I don't allow myself to look back on my old life, but only to look forward into new hope and determination. I believe I am destined to do great things for God. I believe that all of us have a destiny and a purpose to perform here on earth, and I feel that God is preparing me for that designation, that a new life of service and ministry is opening up for me and that in God's timing it will all come to pass. I know that I have been ordained for this work and every day I seek out God and my new life, with joy and happiness. Never giving up on myself, but always seeing the bigger picture, that my life can help others, to be of service, to be a helper and an obedient child of God. I don't know exactly what God has in store, but I believe it is far greater and wider than I can envision. If you are reading this, please today seek God, He will help you, He will guide you, because He is the only one who can. Never give up on God for He never gives up on you.

Never Give Up

Never Doubt

Never Forget

Never Stop

For There Is A God

That Never Gives Up On Us

He Never Doubts Us

He Never Stops Us

We Stop Ourselves

We Turn Aside

We Lose The Dream

We Lose The Vision

Allow God

See God

Meet God

And God Will Turn Your Doubts

You're Fears

You're Limits Inside-Out

It's His Work

Not Us Working Anymore

I love you all so much, go with God, go with freedom and go with joy.